BUILDING YOUR SPIRITUAL TOOLBOX

Laying the Foundation

By Crickett Keeth

Building Your Spiritual Toolbox

By Crickett Keeth

A Personal Note

There have been several women who have built into my life over the years through discipleship. They invested in me, and, as a result, they made a difference in my life of eternal significance. Bonnie was the first woman to disciple me when I was a junior at LSU, and I knew then that I wanted to invest my life in others in the same way she invested in me.

I have found that many people feel inadequate when it comes to discipleship. I often hear comments like, "Someone asked me to disciple her, and I have no idea what to do with her." Or, "I don't know what discipleship is supposed to look like."

This study is a compilation of materials that people have used with me over the years to help me grow spiritually through discipleship. These materials are intended to be transferable so that you can take a lesson and easily go through it with someone else, who, in turn, can take it and teach it to someone else. You will not necessarily use every lesson with everyone you disciple because you will look at each person's needs individually. However, I usually start with this foundation with everyone I disciple to make sure they know how to share it with someone else.

You can find these and other resources to help you disciple others on my website at www.crickettkeeth.com.

BUILDING YOUR SPIRITUAL TOOLBOX

Laying the Foundation

This study is designed to equip you to build into the lives of others. We use a variety of terms for this – equipping, mentoring, discipling. Regardless of the term you may use, one thing is certain – God wants us to invest our lives in the lives of others. Dr. Howard Hendricks challenged us in our leadership class in seminary, "If you want to make a lasting impact with your life, invest it in the lives of others. There is no greater investment." I pray that you will answer that challenge with a resounding, "Yes, I will!" There is no minimum age limit, and there is no maximum age limit. May we be faithful to make eternal investments as we build into the lives of those around us.

Memory verse for the week: Matthew 28:19-20 (Write it below in your favorite version.)

DAY 1: THE MANDATE

So often we hear the word discipleship, and it either intrigues us, or it scares us. Many of you desire to be discipled, while others of you are afraid someone will ask you to disciple her, and you have no idea where to start. This study will give you a solid foundation to stand on in your own walk with the Lord, as well as tools to equip you to equip others to run the race well. Today we begin with the mandate from Jesus Christ to His disciples and ultimately to all of us who choose to follow Christ as His disciples.

LOOKING UPWARD

1. How do you define discipleship?

2. If you were to ask someone to disciple you, what does that mean to you? What are you looking for in a discipleship relationship?

3. Do you have to have a natural affinity for someone in order to disciple her? Explain your answer.

4. What is the relationship between evangelism, followup, and discipleship?

LOOKING TO GOD'S WORD

Matthew 28:16-20

5. Who were the disciples in this passage?

6. Where were they?

7. What observations do you make about them?

8. Why would Jesus begin with the statement, "All authority has been given to Me in heaven and on earth"? Why would that be significant in light of what He was about to tell them?

9. The one command in the "Great Commission" is not "go," but "make disciples." It reads in the Greek, "While you are going, make disciples..." What is involved in making disciples?

10. What relationship does baptizing and teaching have with making disciples?

11. How would His very last words, "Lo, I am with you always, even to the end of the age" encourage them (and us) in making disciples?

LOOKING REFLECTIVELY

- If you have been discipled by someone, how did it impact your life?

- What are some of your fears in discipleship? Ask Him to strengthen you and give you boldness to obey His Word.

- Discipleship is not an option or suggestion, but a command. Are you willing to invest in someone else's life through discipleship? Are you willing to say, "Yes, Lord, I will"? Write out your thoughts about this to the Lord.

DAY 2: THE SCOPE OF THE MANDATE

LOOKING UPWARD

1. What is the difference between making disciples and preaching the gospel, if any?

2. Which do you enjoy doing most – sharing Christ or discipling? Why?

LOOKING TO GOD'S WORD

3. The "Great Commission" is found in each of the four Gospels in different forms and at a different time in the book of John. It is also found in the Book of Acts. Compare and contrast what Jesus tells them in each of these passages concerning His "commission" to them and to us. Answer these two questions with each passage: what does He tell them to do and to what extent does He want them to do it?

Matthew 28:18-20

- What does He tell them to do?

- To what extent?

Mark 16:15

- What does He tell them to do?

- To what extent?

Luke 24:46-49

- What does He want them to do?

- To what extent?

John 20:21

- What does He want them to do?

- To what extent? (This is not explicitly stated, but implied.)

Acts 1:8

- What does He want them to do?

- To what extent?

4. Mark words or concepts that are repeated in the passages? What is emphasized?

5. How are these five passages similar?

6. How do they differ?

LOOKING REFLECTIVELY

- How does your life demonstrate your commitment to making disciples? Are you being obedient to His command? If not, why?

- Are you willing to share Christ with those God places around you?

- Are you willing to disciple others? Begin praying for God to place people around you to share Christ with and to disciple.

- Spend some time meditating on Luke 24:49 – "...until you are clothed with power from on high." We are clothed with power from on high through the Holy Spirit living within us. How should that impact your life? Are you living as if you believe this truth? Journal your thoughts to God.

DAY 3: MULTIPLICATION IN DISCIPLESHIP

The Gospels are a great handbook for discipleship as you study the life of Christ and how He poured His life into twelve men so that they would continue His ministry once He was no longer physically on this earth. Today we will look at the discipleship ministry of Paul and how he multiplied himself into others, following the example of Jesus Christ.

LOOKING UPWARD

1. Why is it important to build into "faithful men (women)"? Does this mean you shouldn't disciple someone who is not faithful or who is struggling in her walk? Explain your answer.

2. Do you have to have the gift of teaching to disciple others? Explain your answer.

LOOKING TO GOD'S WORD

2 Timothy 2:1-6

3. As Paul addressed his disciple Timothy in this letter, list all that Paul admonished Timothy to do.

4. In verse 2, how many levels of discipleship are included here and what are they?

5. What can you conclude from this example in verse 2? What principles for discipleship can you ascertain from this verse?

6. What additional principles for discipleship can you glean from verses 3-6?

7. Why do you think he uses the examples of a soldier, athlete, and farmer here? What is he trying to get across?

8. From this passage, what characteristics are vital to being a good disciple and discipler?

LOOKING REFLECTIVELY

- What are some examples of "affairs of everyday life" (2 Tim 2:4) that have potential to entangle you and hinder you from being a "good soldier"?

- Are you faithful to pass along to others the "things" you've been taught? If not, why?

- Meditate on 2 Timothy 1:7: "For God has not given us a spirit of timidity, but of power and love and discipline." How does this verse give you confidence in discipling others?

DAY 4: FAITHFUL FOLLOWERS

Today we will look at another example of multiplication in Paul's discipleship ministry. In our passage today, Paul is writing to the Thessalonian church. They had been discipled by Paul and had entrusted what they had learned to faithful men and women. The Thessalonian church is a great example of a ministry of multiplication.

LOOKING UPWARD

1. What is the relationship between multiplication and discipleship?

2. Has discipleship taken place if there is no multiplication? Explain.

3. Is multiplication a method of discipleship or an essential element of discipleship? Explain your answer.

LOOKING TO GOD'S WORD

1 Thessalonians 1:2-10

4. What do you observe about the Thessalonians from this passage? List all that you see.

5. How would you summarize a description of the Thessalonians from these verses?

6. What do you observe about Paul from this passage?

7. How many levels of discipleship (multiplication) do you see in this passage? Who are the participants in each level?

LOOKING REFLECTIVELY

- In what areas would you want someone to imitate your life? What kind of example are you setting for others who are watching your life?

- In what areas would you NOT want them to imitate your life?

- The Thessalonians "turned to God from idols to serve a living and true God, and to wait for His Son from heaven, whom He raised from the dead, that is Jesus, who rescues us from the wrath to come" (1 Thess 1:10, NASB 95). Are there any idols in your life that you need to turn from in order to serve the living and true God?

DAY 5: WHAT DOES DISCIPLESHIP LOOK LIKE?

We often are unsure of exactly what we are to do with someone we're discipling. Should I just meet with them and talk about life? Do I teach them? Do we study a book or the Bible together? Do we pray together? Do we just go out for coffee? Discipleship looks different for every person, and the way you go about it with one person may not be the same with another person. In our passage today Paul shows us four roles that are vital to a discipleship relationship. Ask God to show you how you are doing in fulfilling each role in someone's life.

LOOKING UPWARD

1. What is the difference between discipleship and mentoring (if any)?

LOOKING TO GOD'S WORD

1 Thessalonians 2:1-6

2. Describe Paul and his motivation for sharing the gospel. What characteristics stand out to you about Paul and his attitude about sharing the gospel and building into others from this passage? List as many observations as you can.

1 Thessalonians 2:7-12

3. In these verses, Paul describes four "roles" that are important in discipleship. What are they, and what are the characteristics of each role?

> V. 7

> V. 8

> Vs. 9-10

> V. 11

4. What is Paul's goal in discipleship according to verse 12?

5. How would fulfilling these roles help him accomplish this goal? Why would it be important to have all four roles in a discipleship relationship?

LOOKING REFLECTIVELY

- If you are building into someone's life through discipleship, evaluate how you are doing in each of these four roles. Which of these four roles come easiest for you? Which is hardest? Why?

- Take some time to thank God for those who have built into your life spiritually. Pray for them. Write down how God has used them to spur you on in your walk with Him.

"Discipling is done by *someone, not by something*. It is done by *persons, not by programs*. It is accomplished by *individuals, not by institutions*. Technically, discipling is one Christian person imparting his whole life to another, by example, leadership, and relationship. It always involves life transference." [1]

HELPFUL RESOURCES:

Discipleship Essentials by Greg Ogden

Transforming Discipleship by Greg Ogden

Master Plan of Evangelism by Robert Coleman

Tally Ho the Fox! by Herb Hodges

The Lost Art of Disciple-Making by Leroy Eims

Navigator 2:7 Series by NavPress

10 Basic Steps toward Christian Maturity by Campus Crusade for Christ

---

[1] Herb Hodges, *Tally Ho the Fox!* (Germantown, TN: Spiritual Life Ministries, 2001), 70.

WEEK 2: HOW TO BE SURE OF YOUR SALVATION

It is important for every believer to have a solid foundation on which to build. And no matter how long you have been a Christian, it is always good to go back and review "the basics" from time to time. That is where we will concentrate our time these next four weeks – basic follow-up, the foundational tools. We begin with assurance of salvation.

Even though I became a believer at the age of nine, I did not have assurance of salvation until I was a junior in college when a girl on staff with Campus Crusade for Christ took the time to show me in God's Word why I could be assured of my salvation. I begin with this lesson with everyone I disciple because building a strong foundation begins with assurance of salvation. This is adapted from material taught by Campus Crusade for Christ.

Memory verse for the week: John 5:24 (Write it out below in your favorite version.)

DAY 1: THE GOSPEL

LOOKING UPWARD

1. On what is your assurance of salvation based?

2. What role do feelings play in your salvation?

3. What is the relationship between salvation and works?

We will address these questions and others in today's lesson...

LOOKING TO GOD'S WORD

4. Let's begin with two questions used in Evangelism Explosion:

(a) If you were to die tonight, do you know for certain where you would spend eternity?

(b) If God were to ask you why He should let you into heaven, how would you answer?

5. In order to answer that question correctly, let's briefly review the gospel. Write out the main points from the following verses:

Romans 3:23

Romans 6:23a

Romans 6:23b

Romans 5:8; John 3:16

    a. Why do we need a Savior?

    b. What was the motivation behind Christ dying for us?

Ephesians 2:8-9

    a. What is grace?

    b. What are we saved from?

    c. What is faith?

    d. Can you work for your salvation? Why or why not?

    e. In James 2:14-26 James addresses the relationship between faith and works. Some say that Paul and James are saying the exact opposite, but they are not. What exactly is James saying in this passage, and how does it relate to Ephesians 2:8-9?

6. What does faith have to do with receiving Christ as your Savior, and why is faith a necessity?

7. How does one express faith?

8. Why is it important for a believer to have assurance of salvation?

LOOKING REFLECTIVELY

- Are you a sinner?

- Do you need a Savior?

- Have you placed your faith in the One who came to save you from the penalty for your sins?

- If not, what is holding you back?

There is no greater time than now to accept Jesus as your Savior if you have not already done so. One way to express your faith is through prayer. You can put your faith in Him as Savior by expressing with your heart, "Jesus, I know I am a sinner, and I can never be good enough to pay the penalty for my sins. Thank you that you died on the cross for my sins and you paid the penalty for me. I accept your payment, and I put my faith in you and your work on the cross as my Savior. Indwell me now with your Holy Spirit."

- If you have put your faith in Christ, how should you respond to God moment to moment?

- How are you, in reality, responding to Him?

- Write out your thanksgiving to Him for the great gift He has given you.

DAY 2: CHRIST IS IN YOUR LIFE

As a believer, you can be assured of five truths:

1. Christ is in your life.
2. Christ will never leave you.
3. You have eternal life.
4. You became a child of God.
5. Your sins are forgiven.

We will focus on these five truths the rest of this week and next week. Even though you may "know" these things are true, it is important to know where in Scripture these truths are supported. When you become a believer, you begin a new relationship with Jesus Christ as He indwells you through the Holy Spirit. In today's lesson we will focus on the first truth – Christ is in your life.

LOOKING UPWARD

1. How do you know Christ is in your life? Where in Scripture would you go to support it?

LOOKING TO GOD'S WORD

Ephesians 1:13-14 (NASB 95)

> "In Him, you also, after listening to the message of truth, the gospel of your salvation—having also believed, you were sealed in Him with the Holy Spirit of promise, who is given as a pledge of our inheritance, with a view to the redemption of God's own possession, to the praise of His glory."

2. According to these verses, how do you know that Jesus Christ is in your life?

3. What is your responsibility?

4. What does God do once you put your faith in Him as Savior?

5. Notice the Trinity in this passage – God the Father, Son, and Spirit. How is each one involved in our salvation? (List the "who's" and what is said about each one.)

Revelation 3:14-22 – the letter to the church at Laodicea

6. Revelation 3:20 has also been used to support that Christ is in your life once you ask Him to come in. There has been disagreement over this verse concerning the audience to whom this letter was written. Some believe it was addressed to believers because it was originally addressed to the church at Laodicea, and therefore, cannot be a verse that can be used for an evangelistic invitation. Others feel it was written to both believers and nonbelievers. Because of the spiritual condition of the church at Laodicea, it is likely that there were nonbelievers in that church and this verse was used as an invitation to nonbelievers and those who professed to be believers, but in reality were not. I agree with that view.

- In light of that, how would you use this verse to give someone assurance that Christ is in his life?

LOOKING REFLECTIVELY

- What difference does it make in your daily life to know that Christ lives in you? How does it impact you?

- Reflect on these passages and write out some "lessons for life" from these verses:

Romans 8:9-11

Colossians 1:25-27

- Why is "Christ in you, the hope of glory"?

DAY 3: CHRIST WILL NEVER LEAVE YOU

There are disagreements on the issue of eternal security. Some believe that when you sin, Christ leaves you. Or if you choose to turn away from Him, He leaves you. Others (including myself) believe strongly that once **truly** saved, you cannot lose your salvation. Christ will **never** leave you, if you have sincerely put your faith in Him! Today we will look at this issue of eternal security, and how you can know, standing on God's Word, that He will never leave you.

LOOKING UPWARD:

1. How do you know that Christ will never leave you? Where would you go in Scripture to support your answer?

LOOKING TO GOD'S WORD

2. Christ will never leave you, even when you sin. How do these verses confirm this truth?

> **John 10:27-29**

> **Ephesians 1:13-14**

> **Hebrews 13:5b**

3. How many times do you need to receive Jesus Christ as your Savior? Why?

4. What insights do you learn from Hebrews 10:11-14?

5. Perhaps you know someone who started off strong in their Christian faith and then later turned away from the Lord. How do you explain that? Did they "lose their salvation"?

6. Some will use Hebrews 6:1-8 to support the view that one can lose his salvation. How would you handle this passage?

LOOKING REFLECTIVELY

- What difference does it make in your life to know that Christ will never leave you?

- How do you respond when you don't **feel** that Christ is in your life?

- Are you struggling today in your relationship with Christ? Perhaps you are walking in sin and do not feel His presence; or perhaps you are just going through a "dry" time. Write out the above Scriptures and personalize them to your own life. Claim them. Stand on them, not on your feelings.

- Complete the sentence, "God, I feel _____, but your Word says _____."

- Write out a prayer of thanksgiving that He will never leave you.

DAY 4: YOU HAVE ETERNAL LIFE

LOOKING UPWARD

1. The third truth you can be assured of as a Christian is that you have eternal life. How would you define eternal life? When does it begin?

2. How do you **know,** without any doubt, that you have eternal life? What Scriptures do you stand on?

LOOKING TO GOD'S WORD

3. What do you learn about eternal life from Romans 6:23?

4. According to these passages, how do you **know** you have eternal life?

    John 3:36

    John 5:24

    1 John 5:11-15

5. What words stand out to you in 1 John 5:11-15? Look for repetition. Why are these words emphasized?

6. What is our assurance of eternal life based on? (How does Hebrews 5:9 confirm this?

7. How does Jesus define eternal life in John 17:1-3 and who has it?

8. In Luke 10:25-28, a lawyer put Jesus to the test and asked, "What shall I do to inherit eternal life?" Why do you think Jesus handled this question the way He did? Looking at the story that follows about the Good Samaritan, what was the message Jesus was trying to get across to this man concerning eternal life?

LOOKING REFLECTIVELY

- Believing in Jesus Christ is more than an intellectual knowledge of Him. Believing involves an adherence to, trust in. Do you really know Him, or do you just know of Him?

- Spend some time thanking Him for the eternal life He has given you. Ponder what it required on His part to give you eternal life. Write a psalm of praise to Him.

DAY 5: YOU BECAME A CHILD OF GOD

LOOKING UPWARD

1. What are the benefits of being a child of God?

LOOKING TO GOD'S WORD

John 1:12-13

2. How do you become a child of God?

3. List all that is true of "children of God."

4. What does it mean to "receive Him"?

5. According to Romans 8:14-17, what are characteristics and privileges of a child of God?

6. According to Galatians 4:4–7, what took place in order for us to become adopted as "sons"?

7. What are the results of being adopted children of God?

8. How is the Trinity manifested in both the Romans 8 and Galatians 4 passages?

LOOKING REFLECTIVELY

- Are you living like a child of the King, or a child of this world? How do you express gratefulness to your Father for adopting you? Spend some time today thanking Him for what He has done for you. Cry out to your "Abba, Father."

- Some of you do not have fond memories of your earthly father. But God, your heavenly Father, loves you completely and wants to pour out His love on you. What expectations do you have of your heavenly Father?

The fifth truth you can be assured of as a believer is that your sins are forgiven. We will cover this truth in Week 3.

WEEK 3: HOW TO BE SURE YOU ARE FORGIVEN

We will focus our study this week on the fifth assurance we can have as a believer – the assurance of the forgiveness of sins.

Memory verse for this week: Ephesians 1:7 (Write it out below in your favorite version.)

DAY 1: YOUR SINS ARE FORGIVEN

LOOKING UPWARD

1. Are there any sins that are unforgivable? Explain your answer.

LOOKING TO GOD'S WORD

2. Read Colossians 1:13-14. As you observe what God has done for us, make note of the two verb phrases used in verse 13. What does the use of these verbs imply?

3. What is the domain of darkness?

4. How do we appropriate redemption and forgiveness?

5. What observations do you make from Colossians 2:13-14 about your status before coming to Christ?

6. What does it mean that we were "dead in our transgressions"?

7. List all that God has done for us concerning our sins according to the above passage.

8. List your observations from Ephesians 1:5-8. Ask the questions what, why, who, how.

   (For instance, what did He do? What does it mean that He predestined us?)

9. What characteristics/attributes of God are evident in this passage? Describe Him.

10. Is there a difference between redemption and forgiveness? If so, what?

LOOKING REFLECTIVELY

- Are you struggling with guilt from a past sin? Do you believe that He has forgiven you and covered that sin? Or do you still feel you must do penance and beat yourself up for a sin in your past? He has paid the ultimate price for all your sins. It is finished. Your sins are paid for. You may still feel guilty, but walk by faith in God's Word, not by your feelings. God's Word says your sins are forgiven! Your feelings don't change that truth.

- Is there a recurring sin you can't seem to break free from? Ask the Lord to give you victory over that sin in the power of the Holy Spirit living within you. Be accountable to a friend. Stay away from situations that would tempt you to sin. You may want to meet with a counselor to help you walk through this and break free.

- Write or pray a psalm of thanksgiving to Him for all He has done for you.

DAY 2: THE BASIS OF FORGIVENESS

LOOKING UPWARD

1. On what are you basing your forgiveness? Why?

LOOKING TO GOD'S WORD

2. According to these verses, what is the basis of your forgiveness?

    Matthew 26:28

    Ephesians 1:7

    Hebrews 9:13–14

    Hebrews 9:22

    Hebrews 10:19

3. Do works play any role in our redemption according to these verses? Why or why not?

4. Why is there no forgiveness without the shedding of blood? Why is blood necessary?

5. As you read Hebrews 10:10-14, answer the following questions:

    a. Verse 10 begins with "By this will …" Looking back at the context, to what is "this will" referring?

    b. What does sanctification mean?

c. How are we sanctified?

d. When does your sanctification begin and why?

6. According to Hebrews 10:12, 18, why is there no need for continual sacrifices for our sins?

7. According to Hebrews 10:19-25, what do we receive and experience as a result of what Jesus has done for us?

8. As a result, how are we to respond (vv. 22-25)?

9. Why would these imperatives be important for us to do?

LOOKING REFLECTIVELY

- Draw near confidently to God today with a sincere heart in full assurance of faith.

- How would you evaluate your response to God and others in light of what He has done for you?

- In what areas do you need to improve? How will you go about doing that?

- Are you wavering in any area of your faith? "Hold fast the confession of your hope without wavering."

- What are some practical ways in which you can stimulate someone to love and good deeds this week?

- "He who promised is faithful" (Heb 10:23). Write down ways you have seen God's faithfulness in your life recently. Praise Him.

DAY 3: WHY DO I STILL SIN?

Sometimes we think that as a Christian we should no longer sin, and we get discouraged when we continue to see sin in our lives. The longer I walk with the Lord, the more sin I see in my life – often times, sins that are more subtle –pride, jealousy, envy, insecurity, introspection … to name a few.

LOOKING UPWARD

1. What exactly is sin?

2. How does Scripture define sin?

3. Why do you still sin as a Christian? Can you reach a point of sinless perfection on this earth?

LOOKING TO GOD'S WORD

Galatians 5:16-25

4. What is the root issue of sin? What does that mean?

5. What are the two opposing sides in this struggle?

6. Paul instructed the Galatians in verse 16 to walk by the Spirit. How would you know if you are walking in the Spirit or not?

7. As you look over the deeds of the flesh in verses 19-21, how would you divide them into groups or categories? How are they related?

8. As you look over the fruit of the Spirit in verses 22-23, what do they have in common?

9. In what ways do the fruit of the Spirit differ from the deeds of the flesh?

LOOKING REFLECTIVELY

- How have you seen the two opponents battle in your own life?

- Which of the characteristics in verses 19-23 are evident in your life?

- Be honest with God. With what areas of the flesh do you still struggle? Which side is winning the battle in your life – the flesh or the Spirit?

DAY 4: HOW DO I DEAL WITH SIN?

We have established that, as believers, we are forgiven because of Christ's blood that was shed for us. However, as believers, we still sin. So, the question arises, how do I deal with sin? God does not want us to be a slave to sin, but longs for us to be free from sin and its devastating guilt.

LOOKING UPWARD

1. How do you deal with sin in your life?

2. How does it affect your life when you ignore sin and do nothing about it?

LOOKING TO GOD'S WORD

1 John 1:9 (NASB 95)

> "If we confess our sins, He is faithful and righteous to forgive us our sins and to cleanse us from all unrighteousness."

3. What exactly does it mean to confess sin?

4. Are we forgiven because we confess? Why or why not?

5. Why do we need to confess sin if we are already forgiven?

6. Does this verse mean we are only forgiven for the sins we are aware of and specifically confess? Explain your answer.

7. Why do some still feel guilty after they confess their sin?

8. How do the following verses affirm that you are forgiven, regardless of your feelings? What stands out to you from each verse?

Isaiah 53:6

Isaiah 1:18

Psalm 103:12

Romans 4:7–8

Romans 8:1

Colossians 2:13

1 John 2:12

Isaiah 43:25

9. What does it mean that God "will not remember your sins"?

LOOKING REFLECTIVELY

- Are there any unconfessed sins in your life today? If so, write them down on a piece of paper. Then prayerfully confess them to God. Write out 1 John 1:9 and Isaiah 43:25 across the paper. Then tear it up and throw it away. Let it be a visual reminder to you that **ALL** your sins are forgiven (past, present, and future). Thank God for His forgiveness.

DAY 5: WHY NOT GO AHEAD AND SIN ALL I WANT?

LOOKING UPWARD

1. Do you lose your salvation when you sin? Explain your answer. (You may need to look back at Week 2 on Assurance of Salvation.)

2. How does sin affect your relationship with God?

3. If you have salvation by faith, and know you have eternal life, why not just go ahead and sin all you want to?

LOOKING TO GOD'S WORD

4. The Bible gives us several reasons why we shouldn't just keep sinning once we are a Christian. The first reason is found in John 14:15: "If you love Me, you will keep My commandments." Why and how is this true?

5. A second reason we shouldn't just keep sinning once we become a believer is because we will be miserable. Describe the struggle going on within Paul in Romans 7:15-25.

6. What is the solution to this struggle?

7. According to Hebrews 12:6-11, another reason to not continue sinning is because God will discipline you. In what ways does God discipline His children when they sin?

8. Why does God discipline us according to this passage?

9. What other observations can you make from this passage concerning discipline?

LOOKING REFLECTIVELY

- How do you feel when you sin?

- Meditate on Psalm 130. Write out your thoughts from this Psalm. Thank Him for His forgiveness. Don't treat His forgiveness as "cheap grace."

WEEK 4: HOW TO DRAW FROM THE POWER OF THE HOLY SPIRIT

Even though I became a Christian at a young age, I did not understand the ministry of the Holy Spirit in my life until I was a junior in college. I had tried for all those years to live the Christian life in my own strength and found it very difficult. What a difference it made in my life once I understood that the power source for living the Christian life was not my own strength, but the Holy Spirit living within me.

Are you trying to live the Christian life on your own strength, or are you drawing from the power source He has given you? This week our study will focus on the ministry of the Holy Spirit in the life of the Christian. Ask God to teach you from His Word and to reveal to you any areas in which you are not drawing from His power.

Memory Verse for the Week: Ephesians 5:18 (Write it out below.)

DAY 1: WHO IS THE HOLY SPIRIT AND WHY DID HE COME?

LOOKING UPWARD

1. What do you know about the Holy Spirit and His role in the life of the believer?

LOOKING TO GOD'S WORD

2. In John 16:7-14, Jesus gave us insight into who the Holy Spirit is and what His role is. As you look at this passage, answer the following questions concerning the Holy Spirit.

    a. What had to happen first before the Holy Spirit could come to us and why?

    b. What observations do you make about the Holy Spirit in this passage?

c. "He will not speak on His own initiative" (v. 13). What does that imply?

3. According to the following verses, what else does the Holy Spirit do?

Luke 12:11-12

Acts 1:8

Romans 8:26

1 Corinthians 3:16

1 Corinthians 12:7, 11

2 Corinthians 1:21-22

Ephesians 1:13–14

Ephesians 4:30

4. What does a seal imply?

5. What is the purpose of a pledge?

6. What additional observations do you make about the Holy Spirit and His role in the life of a believer from John 14:16-17, 26?

a. How long is the Holy Spirit with you?

b. Where is He today?

c. How is He characterized?

LOOKING REFLECTIVELY

- What especially encourages you from today's verses?

- How have you seen the Holy Spirit clearly at work in your life? How is He at work today?

- Write a prayer of thanksgiving to God for how He is at work in your life.

DAY 2: THE COMMAND TO BE FILLED WITH THE SPIRIT

LOOKING UPWARD

1. What does it mean to be filled with the Holy Spirit? How would you support that with Scripture?

2. How do you become filled with the Spirit?

LOOKING TO GOD'S WORD

Ephesians 5:15-21

3. What are some things we are NOT to do as Christians?

4. What are the positive commands and exhortations Paul gives to the Ephesians in verses 15-18?

5. Why would he contrast being foolish with understanding God's will in verse 17?

6. Why would he contrast being filled with the Spirit with being drunk with wine in verse 18? (What does "dissipation" in the NASB mean?)

7. What are the resulting characteristics of the person who is filled with the Holy Spirit (vs 19-21)?

8. How does John 15:4-5 relate to the Spirit-filled life?

9. What does it mean to abide in Christ? How does one go about abiding in Christ?

Note: When we say "filled with the Spirit," this is not referring to charismatic speaking in tongues. The word "filled" actually means "to be directed and empowered by." To be filled with the Spirit is the same as "abiding in Christ." To be filled with the Spirit is to live in conscience dependence upon Him. Jesus Christ does not want you to try to live the Christian life. He wants to live the Christian life **through** you as you abide in Him.

LOOKING REFLECTIVELY

Scripture commands us to "be filled with the Spirit." It also makes it clear what the Spirit-filled life should look like in a believer.

- Are you edifying other believers with your words and actions or tearing them down?

- Are you making a joyful melody with your heart to the Lord or do you sound like a clanging cymbal?

- Are you always giving thanks for all things or do you tend to be negative?

- Are you willing to submit to one another in the fear of Christ or do you demand your own way? Are you teachable?

- Are you being obedient to God's Word and living as a Spirit-filled believer? If not, what is hindering you? Write out your thoughts to the Lord. Be honest with Him.

DAY 3: THREE TYPES OF PEOPLE

LOOKING UPWARD

1. How do you define a carnal Christian?

2. Does a person become carnal every time he sins? Explain your answer.

LOOKING TO GOD'S WORD

1 Corinthians 2:1-13

3. What impact did the Holy Spirit have on Paul's life (Vs 1-5)?

4. What do you learn about the Holy Spirit from verses 10-13?

1 Corinthians 2:14-3:3

5. How does Paul characterize the natural man in verse 14?

6. Is the "natural man" a believer? Explain your answer.

7. How does Paul characterize the spiritual man in verses 15-16?

8. What does Paul mean in verse 15 when he says, "But he who is spiritual appraises all things, yet he himself is appraised by no man"?

9. How does Paul describe the "men of flesh" in 3:1-3? (The men of flesh are often referred to as "carnal.")

10. Are the "men of flesh" Christians? Explain your answer.

11. How do these three "men" (the natural man, the spiritual man, men of flesh) differ?

12. How does someone become carnal or fleshly?

13. How do you become the "spiritual man"?

LOOKING REFLECTIVELY

- As you look at these three types of people, which one best characterizes your life and why?

- Do you need to make any changes in your life in order to become the spiritual "man"? If so, what needs to change?

DAY 4: CHARACTERISTICS OF THE SPIRIT-FILLED LIFE

LOOKING UPWARD

1. Is being spirit-filled a one-time decision like salvation? Explain your answer.

LOOKING TO GOD'S WORD

2. The content of Colossians 3:12-17 is very similar to what Paul wrote in Ephesians 5:18-21. What similarities do you see in the two passages concerning the Spirit-filled life? Mark any words that stand out or are repeated. Ask yourself, why does Paul emphasize these words?

Colossians 3:12-17 (NASB 95)

"So, as those who have been chosen of God, holy and beloved, put on a heart of compassion, kindness, humility, gentleness and patience;
bearing with one another, and forgiving each other, whoever has a complaint against anyone; just as the Lord forgave you, so also should you.
Beyond all these things put on love, which is the perfect bond of unity.
Let the peace of Christ rule in your hearts, to which indeed you were called in one body; and be thankful.
Let the word of Christ richly dwell within you, with all wisdom teaching and admonishing one another with psalms and hymns and spiritual songs, singing with thankfulness in your hearts to God.
Whatever you do in word or deed, do all in the name of the Lord Jesus, giving thanks through Him to God the Father."

Ephesians 5:18–21 (NASB 95)

"And do not get drunk with wine, for that is dissipation, but be filled with the Spirit, speaking to one another in psalms and hymns and spiritual songs, singing and making melody with your heart to the Lord;
always giving thanks for all things in the name of our Lord Jesus Christ to God, even the Father;
and be subject to one another in the fear of Christ."

3. List the fruit of the Spirit in Galatians 5:22-23.

4. Which of these are also mentioned or implied in Colossians 3:12-17 and Ephesians 5:18-21? Mark them in those passages.

5. From these three passages, how would you characterize a person who is Spirit-filled?

LOOKING REFLECTIVELY

- As you look at the characteristics that Paul challenged the Ephesians and Colossians to live out in their own lives, which qualities are evident in your life today?

- In which areas do you need to grow?

DAY 5: HOW TO WALK IN THE SPIRIT

LOOKING UPWARD

1. When you sin, how can you return to walking in the Spirit?

2. What is the difference between grieving the Holy Spirit (Ephesians 4:30) and quenching the Holy Spirit (1 Thess 5:19)?

LOOKING TO GOD'S WORD

3. Although there is not a step-by step formula in the Bible of how to walk in the Spirit, God gives us clear guidelines in His Word. What do these verses instruct us to do and **why** would they be necessary steps to walking in the Spirit?

   1 John 1:9

   Romans 12:1-2

   1 John 5:14-15

4. According to Ephesians 5:18, why is it not optional for a Christian to be filled with the Spirit?

5. What does Galatians 2:20 have to do with walking in the Spirit and the Spirit-filled life?

LOOKING REFLECTIVELY

I caution you to not look for feelings or emotions to assure you that you are filled (controlled and empowered) with the Holy Spirit. It is by faith alone. He wants this for us, we ask it of Him, and we know, by faith, that He will accomplish His will.

- Are you completely surrendered to God? If not, what is hindering you from surrendering?

- Are you grieving or quenching the Holy Spirit? If so, confess it and yield to His control and draw from His power to live the Christian life.

- Write out Colossians 2:6 in your own words.

Once I understood the ministry of the Holy Spirit in my life and how to walk in the Spirit, my life was transformed. I pray that yours will be too! Draw from His power, not your own.

WEEK 5: HOW TO GROW IN THE CHRISTIAN LIFE

Spiritual maturity takes time. It is a lifelong process in which we grow closer to God as we spend time with Him every day, getting to know Him better. We need to be attentive and responsive to what He is saying to us through His Word and through the prompting of the Holy Spirit. We communicate with Him through our prayers, sharing what's on our hearts. The Navigator ministry uses a wheel diagram to show the principles necessary for Christian growth. There are four spokes in the wheel. The vertical spokes (Bible study and prayer) deal with your relationship with God. The horizontal spokes (fellowship and witnessing) deal with your relationship with others (believers and nonbelievers). This week we will look at each of these four areas. Ask God to show you which areas you need to strengthen in order to grow spiritually and develop a balanced Christian life.

Memory Verse for the Week: 2 Peter 3:18 (Write it here in your favorite translation. I encourage you to memorize verses 17 and 18 if you can.)

DAY 1: TIME IN THE WORD

LOOKING UPWARD

1. How much time do you spend in the Bible (God's Word) each day? How do you spend that time?

2. Why is time in the Bible necessary for spiritual growth? How does it impact your life when you are not in His Word?

LOOKING TO GOD'S WORD

1 Peter 2:2 (NASB 95)

> "Like newborn babies, long for the pure milk of the word, so that by it you may grow in respect to salvation…"

3. How does the "pure milk of the word" help you grow in respect to salvation?

2 Timothy 3:16-17 (NASB 95)

> "All Scripture is inspired by God and profitable for teaching, for reproof, for correction, for training in righteousness; so that the man of God may be adequate, equipped for every good work."

4. What does it mean that "all Scripture is inspired by God"? Why would that make it especially powerful in our lives?

5. List each of the four ways God's Word is profitable in your life. Explain how you have seen Scripture used in each way, either in your own life or someone else's life.

6. What is the difference between reproof and correction?

7. What is the overall purpose of God's Word in our lives?

LOOKING REFLECTIVELY

You cannot grow spiritually if you do not spend time consistently in God's Word, feeding on it, listening to His voice, learning what He desires of you and for you.

- Do you long for the Word like a newborn baby longing for milk? Why or why not?

- What hinders you from spending time in the Word?

- What can you do to overcome those hindrances?

- Will you commit to spending time each day in His Word – reading, studying, or meditating?

- Thank Him for His Word.

- Meditate on the memory verse of the week.

DAY 2: THE IMPORTANCE OF GOD'S WORD

Today we will continue our focus on the importance of being in God's Word. Ask God to give you a longing for His Word.

LOOKING UPWARD

1. How well do you know Scripture? If all of your Bibles were taken away, how much of the Word could you feed on by memory?

LOOKING TO GOD'S WORD

Hebrews 4:12 (NASB 95)

"For the word of God is living and active and sharper than any two-edged sword, and piercing as far as the division of soul and spirit, of both joints and marrow, and able to judge the thoughts and intentions of the heart."

2. What does it mean that the Word of God is . . .?

"living" –

"active"

"sharper than any two-edged sword"

"piercing as far as the division of soul and spirit … "

"able to judge the thoughts and intentions of the heart"

Psalm 119 focuses on the Word and the impact it has on our lives. It is an acrostic poem, divided into twenty-two sections, each one having eight verses. The author of this Psalm is uncertain. Because this is a lengthy passage, we will just look at a few sections. Feel free, however, to study the entire Psalm.

3. As you read Psalm 119:1-24, what other words does the psalmist use for the Word of God?

4. In verses 1-24 and 41-48, list his different responses to the Word. For instance, in verse 14, he says, "I have rejoiced in the way of your testimonies . . . ."

5. According to verses 97-104, how did God's Word impact the psalmist's life?

LOOKING REFLECTIVELY

"The goal is not for us to get through the Scriptures. The goal is to get the Scriptures through us."[2] – John Ortberg

- Meditate on a few of the verses that particularly spoke to your heart today. You may want to look at the entire Psalm.

- Write your own psalm to the Lord concerning His Word and what it means to you.

- Meditate on the memory verse of the week.

---

[2] John Ortberg, *The Life You've Always Wanted* (Grand Rapids, MI: Zondervan, 2002), 188.

DAY 3: TIME IN PRAYER

LOOKING UPWARD

1. How would you describe your prayer life?

2. How does prayer deepen your relationship with God?

LOOKING TO GOD'S WORD

3. What are some principles for prayer that you observe from Philippians 4:6-7?

4. In 1 Thessalonians 5:17, Paul instructs the Thessalonians to "pray without ceasing." What does that mean? How does one pray without ceasing?

5. Paul exhorts the Ephesians in Ephesians 6:18, "With all prayer and petition, pray at all times in the Spirit . . . ". What does it mean to "pray in the Spirit"?

6. What is the difference between prayer and petition (supplication), if any?

7. When a disciple asked Jesus to teach them how to pray, He responded with the prayer recorded in Matthew 6:9-13. What elements did Jesus include in this model of prayer?

LOOKING REFLECTIVELY

- How much time do you spend in prayer each day? How much of that time is spent praying for your needs, and how much time is spent praying for others? How much time is spent praying "kingdom prayers"?

- Is there something you are anxious about today? Take it to the Lord. Tell Him what is on your heart. Pray, ask; give thanks for what He is going to do. Spend some time today using the model of prayer in Matthew 6:9-13.

- Meditate on the memory verse of the week.

Some suggestions to help you pray:

➢ Keep a list of prayer requests and divide requests up per day or several days of the week.

➢ Pray through Scripture.

➢ Pray out loud, or pray together with someone else.

➢ Write out your prayers in a journal.

➢ Pray while you take a walk.

➢ If you are discipling a new believer who is not sure how to pray, spend time with them in prayer. God is not so concerned with the eloquence of our words, as He is with the sincerity of our hearts.

DAY 4: FELLOWSHIP

Spending time with God in His Word and in prayer strengthen our vertical relationship with the Lord. Fellowship and witnessing strengthen our horizontal relationships with people. Today we will look at the importance of fellowship.

LOOKING TO GOD'S WORD

1. What are the exhortations or imperatives found in Hebrews 10:24-25? From this passage, what ingredients are necessary for biblical fellowship?

2. Read Acts 2:42-47. Describe the fellowship among the Christians in the first-century church. What stands out to you about these believers?

3. The Old Testament also encourages us to fellowship with one another. How does Ecclesiastes 4:9-10 encourage us toward fellowship?

4. You may be going to church on Sunday mornings and gathering with other believers for worship. Is that enough to accomplish the purpose of fellowship? Why or why not?

LOOKING UPWARD

5. What is true biblical fellowship?

6. Can a Christian have fellowship with a non-believer? Explain your answer.

7. Is there such a thing as "negative fellowship"? If so, what does it look like?

8. Why is fellowship with other believers a necessity to spiritual growth?

LOOKING REFLECTIVELY

"How inexhaustible are the riches that open up for those who by God's will are privileged to live in the daily fellowship of life with other Christians."
– Dietrich Bonhoeffer

- How are you doing in the area of fellowship with other believers? What changes, if any, do you need to make?

- What is one thing you can do this week to actively fellowship with another believer or group of believers? Initiate it. After the time of fellowship, write down how that time impacted your life.

- Meditate on the memory verse of the week.

DAY 5: WITNESSING

LOOKING UPWARD

1. How does sharing your faith strengthen your relationship with the Lord?

2. What holds you back from sharing your faith?

LOOKING TO GOD'S WORD

3. How do these verses support the importance of sharing Christ with others?

Matthew 4:19

Mark 16:15

Luke 19:10

Acts 1:8

1 Peter 3:15

4. In order to share Christ with others, you must know what to share. We will look at this in detail in a few weeks, but 1 Corinthians 15:3-4 is the gospel plain and simple. What are the main points of the gospel that need to be communicated according to these verses?

5. As you continue reading verses 5-11, list all those to whom Christ appeared.

6. Why are these details of the appearances significant?

7. Describe Paul's attitude toward preaching and sharing the gospel with others in verses 8-11.

8. Paul stated in Romans 1:16 (NASB 95), "For I am not ashamed of the gospel, for it is the power of God for salvation to everyone who believes, to the Jew first and also to the Greek." What observations do you make concerning Paul and the gospel from this verse?

LOOKING REFLECTIVELY

- When was the last time you shared Christ with someone or talked to someone about the Lord?

- Does your life reflect that you are ashamed of the gospel in any way? If so, how?

- Confess your fears to the Lord. Ask Him for boldness. He has given you all that you need in order to share Christ.

- Begin praying for those God has placed in your life who need the Lord. Take the initiative to talk to someone about Christ this week. Ask God to open a door and give you a "divine appointment." Journal about your experience.

- Meditate on the memory verse of the week.

WEEK 6: HOW TO SPEND TIME ALONE WITH GOD

Devotional times or quiet times are vital to our spiritual growth. Seek to spend time alone with the Lord each day in His Word and in prayer. There is no one way to do it, and the method may change as you change seasons in life. The important thing is that you spend time with Him consistently. The purpose of a quiet time is not to do Bible study, although spending time in His Word should definitely be part of your time alone with Him. The purpose of a quiet time is not to just pray, although that also should be part of your quiet time. The purpose of a quiet time is not just a time to confess your sins, although we certainly should include that in our quiet times. But those three things are not the purpose of a quiet time. They are essential ingredients to help us accomplish the main purpose, which is to fellowship with the Lord, enjoying being alone in His presence, getting to know His heart through His Word, and sharing our heart with Him in prayer.

Memory Verse for the Week: Hebrews 4:16 (Write it out in your favorite version.)

DAY 1: THE IMPORTANCE OF A DEVOTIONAL TIME

First we will look at an Old Testament example of meeting with God. Then we will spend the remainder of the week using different methods to help you in spending time alone with the Lord in your devotional or quiet time.

LOOKING UPWARD

1. What do you typically do in your quiet times with the Lord?

2. What keeps you from spending time alone with God each day? What keeps you from spending time in His Word each day?

LOOKING TO GOD'S WORD

3. As you read Exodus 33:7-11, what are some principles you can derive from this passage about spending time alone with God?

   • Where? (v. 7)

- What took place in their time together? (vs. 9-11)

- Is there anything else that stands out to you about this time?

4. What observations can you make from Ecclesiastes 5:1-2 concerning time alone with God? What imperatives did Solomon give?

5. Why do you think Solomon gave those specific imperatives?

6. If Jesus felt the need to get alone with the Father while He was on this earth, how much more should we? What can you learn about time alone with God from Jesus' example in Mark 1:35? You might ask the questions when, where, why, what.

LOOKING REFLECTIVELY

Our days are naturally filled with lots of noise, hurrying from one place and one event to another. We are surrounded by people. To take time away to just sit and enjoy the presence of God is not easy for some, especially in the midst of busyness. Unless we plan for daily times alone with God and in His Word, that time will be pushed aside to make room for all the other pressing voices screaming for our attention. We all have situations that will draw us away from spending time with Him – children, jobs, family responsibilities, other pressing needs – but make time alone with the Lord a priority each day. Spend time in His Word each day, even if it's just to meditate on one verse.

- Are your quiet times something you look forward to each day … or something you HAVE to do … something you can check off your to-do list? What can you do to make your times alone with the Lord more of a delight?

- Will you seek to spend time with the Lord each day? What do you need to do to make that happen?

- Spend some time with Him now. Meditate on the memory verse for the week.

DAY 2: ACTS

For the rest of this week, I will guide you through several ways to have a "quiet time." This is not a Bible study on how to have a devotional time, but rather, you will spend time each day having a quiet time guided by the material for that day. Using variety in our times with the Lord keeps our times with Him fresh, instead of making them seem like a ritual. Ask God to speak to you each day from His Word through the Holy Spirit. Go to Him with a listening heart.

Two important ingredients in our times alone with God are prayer and the Word of God. Prayer is the way we talk to God, and the Word is the means through which God speaks to us. Today, we will focus on the aspect of prayer and how to implement the different forms of prayer into a quiet time. A familiar method that is often used in quiet times is ACTS.

ADORATION

Psalm 29:1-2

- Adoration is not so much thanking God for **what** He has done as it is praising God for **who** He is.
- Worship God for who He is – His attributes and character. You might take each letter of the alphabet and praise Him for that attribute. Or you may take a passage and praise Him for the attributes in the Scripture.
- Write your own psalm of praise to God.

CONFESSION

Psalm 26:2

Ask God to reveal to you any unconfessed sin. Did you speak an unkind word to someone? Did you have a jealous thought? Are you angry about something? Have you gossiped? Do you have a critical spirit? These are a few questions to consider. Be still and ask the Holy Spirit to show you any unconfessed sin.

If you are walking in the Spirit moment by moment, hopefully, you are dealing with sin as soon as you commit it. Keep short accounts with God. Don't let your list of sins build up and then confess them once a week, or once a month. Confess them moment by moment as God reveals them to you. Ask Him to keep you sensitive to the prompting of the Holy Spirit in your life.

THANKSGIVING

1 Chronicles 16:8–12

- What should we be doing according to this passage? List the imperatives.

- Take some time to give thanks for His deeds, what God has done. Write them down.

- Sing to Him, sing praises to Him. Sing a chorus or a favorite hymn, giving thanks. One of my favorite choruses is: "The steadfast love of the Lord never ceases. His mercies never come to an end. They are new every morning; new every morning. Great is Thy faithfulness, O Lord. Great is Thy faithfulness."

- Paul gave instructions to always give thanks for all things (Eph 5:20) and to give thanks in everything (1 Thess 5:18). Does that mean we are to give thanks for even the unpleasant and difficult circumstances in our lives? Explain your answer.

SUPPLICATION

Phil. 4:6 (NASB 95)

> "Be anxious for nothing, but in everything by prayer and supplication with thanksgiving let your requests be made known to God."

Ephesians 6:18 (NASB 95)

> "With all prayer and petition pray at all times in the Spirit, and with this in view, be on the alert with all perseverance and petition for all the saints."

- Supplication means prayer, request, or petition.
- Take some time to pray for others . . . for yourself. Lay your requests before the Lord.
- Pray through the prayers of Paul as you pray for others this week.
  > Ephesians 3:14-21
  > Philippians 1:9-11
  > Colossians 1:9-12

- Pray kingdom prayers. Pray for God's work in the church, in our city, our nation, the world.

- Meditate on the memory verse for the week.

DAY 3: WALKING THROUGH THE TABERNACLE

When I was a college student at LSU, I went on a summer beach project to Myrtle Beach, South Carolina with Campus Crusade for Christ. Each night we gathered together at our house for Bible teaching. One night Rich Bademan shared with us how to have a quiet time by "walking through the Tabernacle." He challenged us to take some extended time that week and find a lonely place on the beach and "walk through the Tabernacle." It revolutionized my quiet times. I don't use this method every day, but when I do, it is always such a sweet time with the Lord. So, today, walk through the Tabernacle with the Lord!

THE OUTER COURT

1. Enter the outer court.

- Enter His courts with thanksgiving and song. (Psalm 100:4)

- Sing praises to Him. A chorus or hymn.

- Praise Him through a psalm. (Psalms 95, 103, 139, 146, 147 are good examples to use.)

- You may want to write your own psalm of praise to Him.

2. Altar of Burnt Offering (Sacrifice) - (Ex 29:10-25) – Aaron and his sons would offer a sacrifice on the altar of burnt offering.

- Romans 12:1-2

- What does it mean to present your body as a living and holy sacrifice? How do you do that?

- Present yourself to the Lord. "Lord, I lay myself on the altar as a living sacrifice. Use me today however you please. I'm yours."

- Is there something hindering you from laying yourself on the altar, giving yourself completely to Him? If so, take time to talk to Him about those issues. Journal. Ask God to remove those hindrances.

- Ask Him to make you willing to present yourself a living sacrifice to Him.

3. Laver for Cleansing (Ex 30:18-21) – Aaron and his sons would wash their feet and hands before entering the tent of meeting so they wouldn't die. This is a time of confession.

- Psalm 139: 23-24

- Psalm 26:2

- Psalm 51:1-3

- 1 John 1:9

- Are there any unconfessed sins in my life?
- Have I spoken unkindly to or about someone? (Eph. 4:29)
- Do I have a critical spirit?
- Am I grumbling and complaining? (Phil. 2:14)
- Is there someone I have not forgiven? (Eph. 4:32)
- Am I causing any dissension or strife within the body of Christ by my actions or words?
- Are my thoughts true, honorable, right, pure, gracious? (Phil. 4:8)
- Do I want my way more than God's way?
- Am I bitter or angry about something? (Eph. 4:31)
- Am I walking in my flesh, or by the power of the Holy Spirit?
- Go before the Lord. Ask Him to search your heart and to reveal any unconfessed sin. Confess it, and turn away from it. He has forgiven you and cleansed you from your sin.

THE INNER COURT – THE HOLY PLACE (Heb. 9:2)

1. Candlesticks on the lampstand (Ex. 25:31-40). The lampstand was made of pure gold with 6 branches. Oil was from beaten olives. The priests would trim the wicks twice a day – morning and evening (Ex. 30:7-8).

- The oil symbolizes the Holy Spirit, the power source.
- Ephesians 5:18 - Be filled with the Spirit.
- Ephesians 3:14-19
- "Lord, take control of my life. I acknowledge that I cannot live the Christian life in my own strength. Empower me through the power of your Holy Spirit."

2. Table of Showbread (Ex. 25:23-30)

- A reminder of God's provision. Jesus is the Bread of life. (John 6:48)
- Phil. 4:19 God provides for us and meets our needs.
- Thank Him for His provisions and answers to prayers.
- Thank Him for what He has done in your personal life. Thank Him for what He has done and is doing in this church and in this ministry.

3. Altar of incense (Exodus 30:1-10)

- Aaron burned fragrant incense on the altar twice a day, and he made atonement on its horns once a year before going into the Holy of Holies.

- Psalm 141:2, Rev 5:8, Rev 8:3-4 (The prayers of the saints are like incense before the Lord.)

- This is the place of intercession and supplication for others. Pray for others, your own personal needs, issues that need to be prayed over, etc. (Phil 4:6)

- What is on your heart today? Take it before Him.

THE INNER COURT – THE HOLY OF HOLIES (Ex.40:3; Heb. 9:3-5)

- Now you're ready to just spend time enjoying being in His presence.
- Psalm 46:10 (KJV) - "Be still and know that I am God."
- Enjoy being in His presence. Sing, journal, study His Word. Be silent. Let Him speak to you through His Word.
- Even though I look at Scripture throughout each section of the Tabernacle, this is where I spend time in His Word. I do my Bible study here, and I ask God to make me attentive and responsive to what He wants to say to me through His Word.
- Linger in His presence. Enjoy the Holy of Holies all day long. Just because you leave your devotional or quiet time does not mean you leave His presence or that your sweet fellowship with Him is over. Continue to enjoy sweet communion with Him throughout the day.

- Meditate on the memory verse for the week.

DAY 4: A THREE-STEP DISCIPLINE

In Bill Hybels' book *Honest to God? Becoming an Authentic Christian*, he talks about how he developed a three-phased life-changing discipline that he uses every day to keep him connected to God.[3] Today, we will use this discipline in our time alone with God.

I. JOURNALING

1. Why is journaling helpful? What does it accomplish?

2. Begin by journaling. Start with the word, "Yesterday…" Bill Hybels explains, "Write a brief description of people you met with, decisions you made, thoughts or feelings you had, high points, low points, frustrations, Bible-reading – anything about the previous day. Then analyze it. Did you make good decisions, or bad decisions? Did you use your time wisely or waste it? Should you have done anything differently?"[4] Evaluate yesterday.

3. Write down what you would like to accomplish today.

---

[3] Bill Hybels, *Honest to God? Becoming an Authentic Christian* (Grand Rapids: Zondervan, 1992), 18.

[4] Ibid., 19.

II. PRAYER

If you have trouble concentrating and staying focused when you pray, write out your prayers in your journal. I often do that and it is encouraging to look back over my prayers throughout the week, and see how God has answered.

Use the ACTS pattern again.

Adoration: Bill Hybels continues, "Each morning after filling my 'yesterday' page, I write a big A on the next page, then spend a few minutes writing a paragraph of praise to the Lord. Sometimes I paraphrase a psalm, or attempt to write a poem. Sometimes I write the words to a praise song, and then sing it quietly in the privacy of my office. Often, I focus on the attributes of God, sometimes listing them all, sometimes meditating on just one. . . Begin to worship God when you pray. Be creative. Experiment. Use choruses and psalms."[5]

Confession: Write out specific sins.

Thanksgiving: In your journal, thank God for specific spiritual, relational, and material blessings.

Supplication: Bill Hybels breaks his prayers into four categories: ministry, people, family, and personal. You can make up your own categories of prayer. Keep a list of what you've prayed for and periodically look back over them to see how God has responded to your prayers. Keep a journal of answered prayers.

---

[5] Ibid., 20-21.

III. LISTENING

Psalm 46:10 (KJV) – "Be still and know that I am God."

Listen and be open to what God wants to say to you. This will not be through an audible voice, but through the prompting of the Holy Spirit as you spend time in His Word and prayer. Bill Hybels suggests four questions to ponder during this time: [6]

    1. What is the next step in my relationship with you, Lord?

    2. What is the next step in the development of my character?

    3. What is the next step in my family life?

    4. What is the next step in my ministry?

You might ask other questions: What is the next step in my vocation? In my dating relationship? In my marriage? In my education? In my retirement?

- Spend time in His Word, being attentive and responsive to His voice through His Word.

- Meditate on the memory verse for the week.

---

[6] Ibid., 25-26.

DAY 5: PRAYING THROUGH A PSALM

Many of the Psalms are David's quiet times, his conversations with God. Some of the psalms were written during times when David was scared, tired, in need, and they express supplication and requests. Other psalms were written to praise God. It is refreshing to take a psalm and pray it back to God, as well as make notes on what speaks to you from the psalmist's words. David's psalms tend to always focus on who God is and what He has done, and brings that to the forefront of our thoughts. Today, pray through Psalm 145 in your time alone with the Lord. Go before Him in awe and worship.

Psalm 145

1. Begin by praying the psalm back to God. For instance, beginning in verse 1, "I will extol You, my God, O King. I will bless your name forever and ever. Lord, You are great and highly to be praised. Your greatness is unsearchable."

2. How have you seen God's greatness in your life?

3. Write down all the attributes of God that are mentioned in this psalm and praise God for them.

4. Make a list of all that God does for us. Thank Him.

5. How did David respond to God? How are we to respond? Ask God to give you the desire to respond in the appropriate way to Him.

6. "All Your works shall give thanks to You, O Lord" (v. 10). Give thanks to the Lord.

7. How have you seen God's grace and mercy and abundant goodness in your life (v. 7)?

8. Write down anything else that stands out to you from this psalm. Perhaps write a psalm of your own to the Lord.

You can develop your own creative ways to spend time alone with the Lord.

- Meditate on the memory verse of the week.

HELPFUL RESOURCES

Chambers, Oswald. *My Utmost for His Highest*. Barbour Publishing, 1963.

Coleman, Mrs. Charles E. *Streams in the Desert*. Zondervan, 1966.

Hybels, Bill. *Honest to God? Becoming an Authentic Christian*. Zondervan, 1992.

Lotz, Anne Graham. *Daily Light for Every Day*. Thomas Nelson, 1998.

Rhodes, Tricia McCary. *The Soul at Rest: A Journey Into Contemplative Prayer*. Bethany House, 1996.

Young, Sarah. *Jesus Calling*. Thomas Nelson, 2004.

WEEK 7: HOW TO STUDY THE BIBLE

It is essential to spiritual growth to spend time daily in God's Word. There are a variety of ways to do this, depending on what your goal is. There is no one way to do Bible study that fits everyone and every season of life. What is effective while you're working outside of the home may not be as effective when you are at home with small children. Find what works best for you in your particular season.

Memory Verses for the Week: 2 Timothy 3:16-17 (Write it out in your favorite version.)

DAY 1: THE SEVEN QUESTION METHOD

Dr. Howard Hendricks first introduced me to nine application questions to ask when studying a passage when I took his Bible Study Methods Class at Dallas Seminary. You can read more about this in his book *Living by the Book*. I have adapted those questions for my own personal study.

Read 1 Timothy 6:6-21 and answer the seven questions listed below. Note that some of the questions will not be applicable to every passage.

1. Is there a warning to consider?

2. Is there a sin to avoid or confess?

3. Is there a command to obey?

4. Is there a promise to claim?

5. Is there a prayer to personalize?

6. What do I learn about God/Jesus/the Holy Spirit from this passage?

7. So what? How can I apply this passage to my life? What do I need to change or implement in my life as a result of this passage? Write out some life lessons to apply.

- You can ask these questions on any passage you read. Just remember that not all the questions will apply to every passage.

- Meditate on the memory verses of the week.

DAY 2: INDUCTIVE BIBLE STUDY: OBSERVATION

Howard Hendricks, in his book *Living by the Book*, uses a three-step approach to Bible study. Today we will look at Step One: Observation. Our passage this week is 1 Timothy 6:6-21.

1. Begin by reading the passage all at once. For your convenience, I have printed it here in the NASB 95 version. Mark it, circle words, draw arrows, whatever would help you to study this passage.

1 Timothy 6:6–21 (NASB 95)

6 "But godliness actually is a means of great gain when accompanied by contentment.

7 For we have brought nothing into the world, so we cannot take anything out of it either.

8 If we have food and covering, with these we shall be content.

9 But those who want to get rich fall into temptation and a snare and many foolish and harmful desires which plunge men into ruin and destruction.

10 For the love of money is a root of all sorts of evil, and some by longing for it have wandered away from the faith and pierced themselves with many griefs.

11 But flee from these things, you man of God, and pursue righteousness, godliness, faith, love, perseverance and gentleness.

12 Fight the good fight of faith; take hold of the eternal life to which you were called, and you made the good confession in the presence of many witnesses.

13 I charge you in the presence of God, who gives life to all things, and of Christ Jesus, who testified the good confession before Pontius Pilate,

14 that you keep the commandment without stain or reproach until the appearing of our Lord Jesus Christ,

15 which He will bring about at the proper time—He who is the blessed and only Sovereign, the King of kings and Lord of lords,

16 who alone possesses immortality and dwells in unapproachable light, whom no man has seen or can see. To Him be honor and eternal dominion! Amen.

17 Instruct those who are rich in this present world not to be conceited or to fix their hope on the uncertainty of riches, but on God, who richly supplies us with all things to enjoy.

18 Instruct them to do good, to be rich in good works, to be generous and ready to share,

19 storing up for themselves the treasure of a good foundation for the future, so that they may take hold of that which is life indeed.

20 O Timothy, guard what has been entrusted to you, avoiding worldly and empty chatter and the opposing arguments of what is falsely called "knowledge"—

21 which some have professed and thus gone astray from the faith.
Grace be with you."

2. Make as many observations as you can by asking these questions of observation. Just make observations, don't interpret yet. What do you see? Use the Laws of Structure on the next page to also guide you concerning things to look for.

What? What is it about? What are the issues?

Who? Who is the author? To whom is he writing?

When?

Where?

Are there any **contrasts?**

Are there any words, phrases, or concepts that are **repeated?**

Any **progressions**? (from small to great, or great to small)

Names of God?

We will continue our study of this passage tomorrow as we move into interpretation.

LAWS OF STRUCTURE

(Adapted from Robert Traina's book *Methodical Bible Study*) [7]

1. Comparison – the association of like things.

2. Contrast – the association of opposites.

3. Repetition – the reiteration of the same terms, phrases, clauses, etc.

4. Continuity – the repeated use of similar terms, phrases, clause, etc.

5. Continuation – the extended treatment of a particular aspect.

6. Climax – the arrangement of material in such a way as to progress from the lesser to the greater and ultimately to the greatest.

7. Cruciality – the utilization of the principle of the pivot. The subject matter is arranged so that it turns around or upon some one factor.

8. Interchange – the exchanging or alternation of certain elements.

9. Particularization and Generalization – the movement from the general to the particular, and from the particular to the general.

10. Causation and Substantiation – the progression from cause to effect and from effect to cause.

11. Interrogation – the use of a question or problem followed by its answer.

---

[7] Robert A. Traina, Methodical Bible Study (Grand Rapids: Zondervan, 2002), 50-52.

DAY 3: INDUCTIVE BIBLE STUDY: INTERPRETATION

Today we will look at Step Two: Interpretation. As you look at the observations you made yesterday, begin to ask interpretation questions. What does this mean? Why did he say this? How is this true? How do I do this? How does this work? Why is he emphasizing these words or phrases? Use the following questions to guide you through interpretation of the passage.

1. Why is Paul saying these things to Timothy?

2. In verse 6, what is godliness?

3. What did Paul mean when he said, "godliness actually is a means of great gain when accompanied by contentment"? How is that true?

4. Are there any contrasts? What might be Paul's purpose in using contrast here?

5. What words are repeated? Why do you think he repeats and emphasizes these words?

6. How would you define contentment?

7. How does wanting to get rich tempt you?

8. How does it lead to destruction and ruin?

9. I got you started. Now you take it from here! Write down your own interpretation questions and answers. This is where you may want to consult a commentary. Sometimes you will come across a passage where scholars disagree on the interpretation. (For example, issues concerning the end times.) Ask the Holy Spirit to guide you and give you understanding as you interpret the Scripture.

DAY 4: INDUCTIVE BIBLE STUDY: APPLICATION

Today we will do Step Three: Application. So what? How does it impact my life? What should I do? What **will** I do as a result of this passage? How can I apply it to my life personally? You may also want to look back at the seven questions from Day 1 of this week.

1. What are some lessons for life from this passage?

2. What are some things you know God wants you to do in your life as a result of studying this passage?

3. How will you implement those things practically in your life?

DAY 5: CORRELATION

Correlate the passage to what other Scripture says about the same subject. You may take a word, like contentment, and look at the cross references on contentment. What do you learn about contentment from these other passages? Or take godliness and do the same thing. Or material riches ... What does the Word say about these things elsewhere in Scripture?

Your assignment today is to take one or more of these words and cross reference it. You can use the cross-references in the margin of your Bible, or your concordance at the back of your Bible. You may choose to use a separate concordance or a topical Bible (like Naves). Write down what you learn about it, how does it correlate to the 1 Timothy 6 passage? Does it support it, or give a different viewpoint? How can you apply it to your life?

There are a number of ways in which you can spend time in God's Word. Here are some suggestions:

> Read through the Bible in a year. You can download guides for doing this online.
> Read through a book of the Bible paragraph by paragraph or chapter by chapter. Take notes on what God is saying to you. Focus on how you can apply the Word to your own life.
> Use a monthly reading plan such as Daily Walk (available from the Navigators, P.O. Box 20, Colorado Springs, CO 80901).

SUGGESTED RESOURCES FOR BIBLE STUDY:

Hendricks, Howard. *Living by the Book*. Chicago: Moody Press. 1991.

www.Soniclight.com – Read or download for free the expository notes of Dr. Thomas Constable, a Bible exposition professor at Dallas Theological Seminary. This is an excellent resource for further study.

www.Bible.org – Find various resources on this website to help you study.

www.biblegateway.org – Also another helpful website to help you study the Word of God

It is also recommended that you have access to a good topical Bible (like Nave's), a Bible dictionary (Easton's, Harper's, or Eerdmans are all good), and a good concordance (Cruden's is good).

A good commentary set is *The Bible Knowledge Commentary* (OT and NT editions). Edited by John Walvoord and Roy B. Zuck. Victor Books. 1985.

WEEK 8: HOW TO DEVELOP YOUR SHAPE

Each one of us has a unique God-designed **SHAPE**, which stands for **S**piritual gifts, **H**eart, **A**bilities, **P**ersonality, and **E**xperience. This material is adapted from the SHAPE material at Saddleback Community Church in Lake Forest, California. This week we will focus on these five areas and how they can sharpen our understanding of how God is preparing us for serving Him. Ask God to clearly show you how He has uniquely shaped you for His purpose.

Memory Verse for the Week: 1 Peter 4:10 (Write it here in your favorite version.)

DAY 1: SPIRITUAL GIFTS – WHAT ARE THEY?

We begin with the "S" - spiritual gifts. There are four key passages on spiritual gifts. We will spend today and tomorrow looking at these four passages. However, no one passage gives an all-inclusive list of all the gifts.

LOOKING UPWARD

1. Why do you think that no one passage includes all the spiritual gifts?

2. What do you know about spiritual gifts?

LOOKING TO GOD'S WORD

Romans 12:3-8

3. List the gifts that Paul mentions in verses 6-8, along with any description or manner in which they should be used.

4. Why do you think Paul precedes the list of gifts with the admonition to everyone in verse 3 "not to think more highly of himself than he ought to think"?

5. What observations can you make concerning spiritual gifts from this passage?

Ephesians 4:11-13

6. List the gifts mentioned in this passage.

7. What is the purpose of these specific spiritual gifts?

8. What is the ultimate purpose of our spiritual gifts?

1 Peter 4:10-11

9. List the gifts mentioned in this passage and the manner in which they should be used.

10. What does Peter give as the purpose of spiritual gifts?

11. As you look over the lists of gifts from these three passages, is there a gift you don't understand or exactly know what it is? If so, do some research to try to find out what it is and how it should be used today.

LOOKING REFLECTIVELY

- Are you aware of your spiritual gift(s)? Are you using them to serve the body of Christ? If not, why?

- Are you serving the body in your own strength or by the strength which God supplies? How would you know?

- Thank Him for the spiritual gifts He has given you, even if you are not sure yet what those gifts are.

- Meditate on the memory verse for this week.

DAY 2: SPIRITUAL GIFTS - WHY DO WE HAVE THEM?

Today we will continue our look at spiritual gifts.

LOOKING TO GOD'S WORD

1 Corinthians 12:4-31

1. List the gifts mentioned in this passage (Vs 8-10, 28).

2. Who gives us our particular spiritual gift(s) according to verse 11 and how does He determine the gift(s)?

3. What words are repeatedly used in this passage? Why does Paul emphasize these words? What is he trying to get across to the Corinthians?

4. What observations do you make about spiritual gifts from this passage?

5. According to 2 Timothy 1:11, what did Paul consider to be his spiritual gifts?

LOOKING REFLECTIVELY

6. What do you believe to be your spiritual gifts and why?

7. What do you enjoy doing? What energizes you?

8. What do others say are your spiritual gifts?

9. Here are some suggestions to help you discover and develop your spiritual gifts.

A. Examine yourself.

Past: Begin by considering any areas of service in the past where you sensed that the Lord was working through you to accomplish His desire. In other words, what areas of ministry have given you great joy and a sense of satisfaction as you have served? What specific activities gave you the greatest joy?

Present: In what ministries are you currently involved? Are you energized and challenged? Are you highly motivated to give it your best? Do you enjoy a sense of accomplishment when you finish a task?

Future: What are your desires for the future and where can you envision yourself serving? To what ministries are you attracted?

B. Take a spiritual gift assessment.

I don't necessarily think this is the best way to determine your spiritual gifts because every assessment tends to come out differently, depending on how you interpret the questions or depending on the mood you're in when you take the test. I would not rely solely on the assessment, but it can be used along with the questions above as a tool to help you determine your gifts. A good assessment can be found at www.churchgrowth.org and it's free.

C. Evaluate your effectiveness.

Is a ministry opportunity a good fit for your gifts? When do you sense that your service has made a contribution to the body of Christ? What is an area in which you have served but did not feel comfortable or feel that you served well? That is probably not the area of your spiritual giftedness. If you're not sure of your gift, make a short term commitment to serve in an area of need to see if it is indeed an area in which you are gifted.

DAY 3: HEART

We have looked at the "S" of SHAPE – spiritual gifts. Today we will look at the "H" – heart. Just because you are gifted in an area does not mean that you are going to be fulfilled by using that gift in any arena. There are other factors that need to be taken into consideration in determining your area of ministry.

LOOKING UPWARD

1. For what area of ministry do you have a heart?

LOOKING TO GOD'S WORD

2. According to Luke 19:10, for whom did Jesus have a heart?

3. From these verses, for what areas would you say Paul had a heart?

   Acts 20:24

   Romans 15:20

   Galatians 2:8

LOOKING REFLECTIVELY

4. What group of people do you have the greatest concern for or interest in? For instance, it may be children, senior high, young marrieds, inner city, senior adults, just to give you a few examples.

5. What do you enjoy doing? Some examples would be counseling, music, congregational care, evangelism, discipleship, sports, hospitality, administration, teaching, etc.

6. With which do you prefer working?

    Things   Information   People

7. What are some of the most meaningful things you have done in your life; things that gave you a great sense of satisfaction or fulfillment?

8. In conclusion, for what and whom do you have a heart? Are you serving in that area?

- These God-given motivations serve as an internal guidance system for your life. They determine your interests and what will bring you the most satisfaction and fulfillment. They also motivate you to pursue certain activities.

- Journal your thoughts concerning the area or areas to which you are drawn. Ask God to lead you in how to serve in these areas.

DAY 4: ABILITIES

The "A" in SHAPE stands for abilities or natural talents. We need to understand our abilities, because God wants us to use our God-given natural talents and abilities for His glory. Some of you may know what your abilities are and are already putting them to good use. Others of you may not be aware of your talents; or you may be unwilling to acknowledge that you have talents. However, God wants you to use your talents and abilities for Him and for His glory.

LOOKING UPWARD

1. What do you feel you are "naturally" good at?

LOOKING TO GOD'S WORD

2. According to Mark 6:1-3, what were some of Jesus' natural abilities?

3. According to Acts 18:3-4, what were Paul's abilities?

4. Write out 1 Corinthians 10:31 in your own words.

LOOKING REFLECTIVELY

- What are you naturally good at? What comes easy for you?

- What is your current vocation or hobby? Does it come easily for you?

- What are some other skills that you have experience in?

- What do you believe to be your strongest natural abilities or talents?

- Are you using your natural abilities for His glory?

- Meditate on the memory verse of the week.

DAY 5: PERSONALITY AND EXPERIENCES

PERSONALITY

You were born with your personality. For those of you who are moms, you recognize early on the unique personality of your children. Personality is the way you express yourself. Some are outgoing and talkative. Others are shy and quiet. Some love to be with people all the time. Others crave time alone. Some love to be in control. Others are content to be followers. Some get uptight with change; others are laid back, flexible, and don't get upset easily.

LOOKING UPWARD

1. What are the benefits to being aware of your temperament and personality?

LOOKING TO GOD'S WORD

2. How would you describe Paul's personality from Galatians 1:13-14?

3. How does Galatians 1:15-16 encourage you?

4. What stands out to you as you read Psalm 139:13-16, especially as it relates to the way God made you?

LOOKING REFLECTIVELY

- Do you struggle with how God has made you? Do you give Him thanks for the way He has made you, or are you discontent with His "creation"? Be honest with God, but recognize that He has skillfully formed you in your mother's womb.

- You are energized in one of two ways. You may be energized by being with people (extroverts) or by being alone (introverts). Are you more extroverted or introverted? To help you determine your tendencies, circle which words or phrases best describe what you prefer to do? If you're in the middle, mark an X in the middle. (This material is taken from *The Intentional Woman*, written by Carol Travilla and Joan C. Webb, © 2002, Used by Permission of NavPress, All Rights Reserved. www.navpress.com.)

EXTROVERT

I am recharged by:

Interaction

Activity

Working with a team

Conversation

Focusing on what is happening around me

Knowing what others are doing

INTROVERT

I am recharged by:

Being alone

Contemplation

Working alone or one-on-one

Writing

Focusing on what is happening inside

Knowing the idea behind the action

- Are you more motivated to work with people or on tasks?

- Do you like to be in charge or would you rather be a follower? An initiator or responder?

- If you are interested in learning more about your personality type, you can take advantage of some free online resources.

  a. You can take the Keirsey Temperament Sorter-II free online at www.advisorteam.org. They will ask you a series of questions and then email you a report.

  b. You can also take a different personality assessment online at http://www.humanmetrics.com/cgi-win/JTypes2.asp.

  c. The DISC profile is not free, but a good resource. You can take the DISC assessment at www.internalchange.com/disc_profile.

- The next page is a handout with the four major temperaments. We are typically a mix of the four types, but one temperament is usually dominant.

LaHaye Temperaments

(Compiled from *Personality Plus* by Florence Littauer and
Spirit-Controlled Temperament by Tim LaHaye)

The Popular Sanguine
- Strengths: Extrovert, the talker, the optimist, life of the party, appealing personality, enthusiastic and expressive, makes friends easily, exciting.
- Weaknesses: No follow-through, doesn't take himself seriously, talks too much, self-centered, disorganized, fickle (no one loves you more when they're with you and forgets you faster when you're out of sight).

The Perfect Melancholy
- Strengths: Introvert, the thinker, deep, thoughtful, analytical, serious, purposeful, talented and creative, detail conscious, orderly and organized, neat and tidy, perfectionist, economical
- Weaknesses: Easily depressed, low self-image, the pessimist, procrastinates, puts unrealistic demands on others, sensitive, easily hurt.

The Powerful Choleric
- Strengths: Extrovert, the doer, the optimist, born leader, strong-willed and decisive, goal oriented, organizes well, delegates work, thrives on opposition, excels in emergencies.
- Weaknesses: Rationalizes his weaknesses, compulsive workers, must be in control, doesn't know how to handle people, right but unpopular.

The Peaceful Phlegmatic
- Introvert, the watcher, the pessimist, easiest to get along with, the "learned leader," low-key personality, easy-going, calm, cool, collected, patient, administrative, mediates problems, has many friends, a good listener.
- Not exciting or enthusiastic about anything, resists change, seems lazy, appears wishy-washy, indecisive.

The Phlegmatics and Melancholys are introverted, pessimistic, soft-spoken. They analyze.

The Sanguines and Cholerics are outgoing, optimistic, outspoken. They lead.

The Phlegmatics and Sanguines are relationship oriented.

The Cholerics and Melancholys are goal oriented.

We usually have a dominant temperament but are a mixture of several. Which ones best describe you?

EXPERIENCES

So much of our readiness to serve others grows out of a wise response to the life experiences that have been sovereignly woven into our past. By taking time to pay attention to these experiences, we can become alert to opportunities we may have to minister to others who are experiencing the same thing.

LOOKING TO GOD'S WORD

5. According to 2 Corinthians 1:3-4, how does God use our difficult experiences or "afflictions"?

6. What are some of the painful experiences Paul faced?

     2 Corinthians 11:23-27

     2 Corinthians 12:7

7. What was Paul's attitude toward His experiences according to these verses?

     2 Corinthians 12:9-10

     Philippians 4:11-13

LOOKING UPWARD

8. Look over the list of life experiences below and check those you have been through. Be available to walk alongside other women who are struggling in those areas.

____ Death of your husband

____ Divorce or marital separation

____ Marital problems

____ Death of a close family member or friend

____ Remaining single

____ Your own illness or injury

____ Losing a close friendship

____ Fired from your job, or spouse out of work

____ Dissatisfied with your current job

____ Having a husband who travels a great deal

____ Retirement – you or your husband

____ Major change in a family member's health

____ Pregnancy

____ Unwanted pregnancy

____ Miscarriage

____ Inability to have children; adoption

____ Older parents moving into your home

____ Aging parents

____ Son or daughter leaving home

____ Problems with children

____ Trouble with in-laws

____ Unresolved bitterness within your family

9. Family background – How can God use your family background to help you minister to others?

10. Look at your spiritual journey.

    A. What life situations has God used to prepare you to minister to others (difficulties, pain, failure)?

    B. What are some of your accomplishments and significant events?

    C. What experiences do you have in ministry?

LOOKING REFLECTIVELY

- What is your SHAPE and how does your SHAPE help you determine possible ministry direction?

RESOURCES

Carbonell, Mels, PhD. *What Makes You Tick ... And What Ticks You Off!* Blue Ridge, Georgia: Uniquely You Resources, 1997.

Inrig, Elizabeth. *Release your Potential.* Chicago: Moody Press, 2001.

Rima, Samuel D. *Leading from the Inside Out: The Art of Self-Leadership.* Grand Rapids, MI: Baker Books, 2000.

Stowell, Joseph M. *Loving Christ: Recapturing Your Passion for Jesus.* Grand Rapids, MI: Zondervan, 2000.

TerKeurst, Lysa. *Leading Women to the Heart of God: Creating a Dynamic Women's Ministry.* Chicago: Moody Press, 2002.

WEEK 9: HOW TO SHARE YOUR FAITH

Do you find it easy to share your faith? For many of us, it is not. It takes us out of our comfort zones. We fear rejection or being misunderstood – especially in today's world in which there is a growing dislike for Christianity. Yet, if we are going to be obedient to Christ, we must share the gospel with others. This week we are going to look at the motivation and heart behind sharing your faith, as well as a variety of ways to make Him known to others. This will include developing a gospel presentation that you are comfortable with, developing your personal testimony, and leading evangelistic Bible studies with neighbors or coworkers. You may be a little uncomfortable about this week, but don't be. Remember, this study is designed to equip you for ministry to others. You are building your spiritual toolbox. Be ready for any opportunity God places before you to share your faith with someone else. Ask God to take away your fears in this area.

Memory verse this week: 1 Peter 3:15 (Write it out here in your favorite version.)

DAY 1: THE GOSPEL

LOOKING UPWARD

1. When was the last time you shared Christ with someone?

2. What holds you back from sharing your faith? What are your fears?

3. If you were asked to share your faith with someone right now, what would you include? Without looking at notes or looking ahead in this lesson, write down what you would include in a gospel presentation. What are the key truths that you would need to communicate? What Scripture would you use? (You can use your Bibles, but don't look at notes☺).

LOOKING TO GOD'S WORD

There are a number of effective gospel presentations – The Four Spiritual Laws, the Navigator's Bridge illustration, Evangelism Explosion, the Roman Road. Some are short and to the point; others are longer. But they all communicate the same key points. Today we will focus on those key truths that must be communicated in sharing the gospel.

4. We looked at the gospel as presented in **1 Corinthians 15:1-5** in Week 5, but we will look at it again today by way of review. What are the main points of the gospel communicated in this passage?

5. Below are key verses that explain the gospel. Write out the key truth from each verse:

John 3:16

John 10:10b

Romans 3:23

Romans 6:23

Isaiah 53:6

Romans 5:8

Ephesians 2:8-9

John 1:12

John 5:24

Romans 10:9-10, 13

Revelation 3:20

6. Why is it not enough to just **know** these truths intellectually?

7. How would you explain to someone how to accept Jesus as their Savior?

LOOKING REFLECTIVELY

- Take some time to ponder the truths of the gospel. Thank Him for all that He has done to bring about your salvation.

- Pray for those you know who do not know the Lord.

- Pray for an opportunity to talk to someone about Christ this week.

- Meditate on the memory verse for the week.

DAY 2: THE MOTIVATION

What is your motivation for sharing the gospel? Is it out of compassion for the lost? Or is it out of guilt or a sense of obligation? Do you experience great joy in sharing Christ, or do you feel a sense of dread or fear? I have found that I am quick to come up with excuses for not sharing my faith, but when I step out in faith and do it, I love it! Why don't I do it more??? For me, fear of rejection paralyzes me, and I don't like being stretched. But if I am serious about being a devoted follower of Jesus Christ, I must be faithful to share the gospel with others. That doesn't mean we must go out and knock on doors, or walk up to strangers in the mall. I believe that if we are willing and available and asking God for opportunities, He will bring people across our paths. Will you be sensitive to the leading of the Holy Spirit? Will you be available and willing to take the initiative to share Christ in the power of the Holy Spirit when God places someone in your life?

Today we will look at the proper motivation for sharing Christ with others.

LOOKING UPWARD

1. What is your motivation for sharing Christ?

LOOKING TO GOD'S WORD

2 Corinthians 5:14-21

2. Paul clearly presents the gospel in these verses. Write down the points of the gospel he presents here.

3. What does it mean that "the love of Christ controls us" (NASB) in verse 14?

4. In verse 16 what does Paul mean that "from now on we recognize no man according to the flesh"?

5. Describe the person who is "in Christ."

6. What role has God given to us now that we are in Christ? What does that role look like in a practical sense today?

7. What do you learn about God and Jesus in this passage?

LOOKING REFLECTIVELY

- How seriously do you take the ministry of reconciliation and being an ambassador for Christ? How do you represent Him to the world?

- Write out your thoughts to the Lord concerning what He has done for you and the ministry to which He has called you.

- Ask God to give you a compassion for the lost, a heartfelt desire to share Christ with the world. Write out a prayer to Him about this.

- Meditate on the memory verse of the week.

DAY 3: THE AVAILABILITY

Are you available to be used by God to share the gospel? Are you sensitive to the prompting of the Holy Spirit? You don't have to be an eloquent speaker like Billy Graham to share the gospel. God is looking for willing, available hearts. Today we will look at the example of how God used Philip to share the gospel.

LOOKING UPWARD

1. What are some ways to initiate a conversation about Christ or bring a conversation around to spiritual things?

LOOKING TO GOD'S WORD

Acts 8:1-6

2. What was the setting of this chapter? What had just happened and what was going on now?

3. What stands out to you about Philip in this passage?

Acts 8:25-40

4. How was Philip directed by the Lord to the Ethiopian eunuch?

5. What excuses might he have made for not going?

6. How did Philip initiate a conversation with the Ethiopian eunuch?

7. What observations do you make about the Ethiopian eunuch?

8. How did he respond to what Philip shared with him? How did his life change?

9. What character qualities do you see in Philip from this passage? Describe him.

10. What are some principles for sharing your faith that you can glean from this passage?

For Deeper Study: Look at John 3 (Jesus and Nicodemus) and John 4 (Jesus and the Samaritan woman). Write down principles for sharing your faith from these examples.

LOOKING REFLECTIVELY

- Are you purposefully looking for opportunities to share your faith?

- Are you sensitive to the Holy Spirit's prompting in your life to share Christ with someone He has brought across your path?

- Are you moving conversations with non-believers toward spiritual things?

- Are you willing to say, "Lord, I am available"? Journal your thoughts.

- Meditate on the memory verse for the week.

DAY 4: YOUR PERSONAL TESTIMONY

Your personal testimony can be one of the most valuable tools you have in sharing your faith with someone else. People can identify with personal stories and the reality of how Christ has changed your life. But do you have your testimony thought out in an organized way? There are times you will be able to go into as much detail as you want; but there will be other times you will have time constraints in sharing. Today our purpose is to help you write out your testimony in a **concise**, organized manner. Once you have it written out and you know the key points, then you can adapt it to any situation.

LOOKING UPWARD

1. Why would it be beneficial to have your personal testimony written out and thought through in an organized manner?

2. If you have not done this, what has hindered you?

LOOKING TO GOD'S WORD

Before you begin writing out your testimony, we will begin with looking at Paul's testimony in Acts 9. As you read, write down details of Paul's testimony under each of these three areas and then answer the following questions:

I. His life before salvation (Acts 9:1-2)

3. How would you characterize his life at this point?

II. How he came to saving faith in Christ (Vs. 3-19)

4. What question did the Lord ask Saul? Why do you think He asked this particular question?

5. What question did Saul ask the Lord? Why do you think Saul addressed Him as "Lord"?

6. How did Paul express "faith" in the Lord in this passage?

7. What do you observe about Ananias? What stands out to you about him?

8. In verses 15-16, the Lord discloses his purpose for Saul (Paul). What was it?

9. How did God use Ananias in Paul's life according to verses 17-19?

III. His life after he came to Christ (Vs. 19-31)

10. How did Saul's life change? What did he now have a passion to do?

11. What hardships did Saul face now as a follower of Christ?

12. What stands out to you from Saul's testimony, perhaps something you had not noticed before?

LOOKING REFLECTIVELY

Now it's your turn. Starting today and continuing throughout the week, work on writing your testimony. Begin with prayer, asking the Lord to clearly guide you, to point out important circumstances and people that brought you to a saving faith. Some of you (like me) came to Christ at an early age, and so there is not much to write in the "before" section. In this case, share how you came to Christ, but focus on how you came to the point of being under the lordship of Christ and how your life has changed. Paul's testimony was dramatic, but a testimony doesn't have to be dramatic in order to be effective!

To help you get started, I have included a testimony worksheet for you on the next pages. This worksheet will help you organize your thoughts. You may want to pair off with someone in your small group and work on this together. Spend time each day this week working on your testimony and writing it out. Next week we will share our testimonies with each other in our small groups.

Share your testimony with someone who may not know the Lord or who is not walking with the Lord. Then write down your thoughts, how it was received, what God taught you through sharing your testimony.

TESTIMONY WORKSHEET

I. What was your life like before you trusted Jesus Christ or totally committed your life to Him?

A. What were your attitudes, needs, problems?

B. What did your life revolve around? What was most important to you?

C. How did you look for security, peace of mind, happiness? How did you find your activities unsatisfying?

II. How did you come to trust Christ or how did you come to give Him complete control of your life?

A. What were the circumstances surrounding your conversion to Christ/lordship?

B. How did you receive Christ or give Him control of your life?

C. What barriers did you experience?

D. What was the turning point for you?

III. What happened after you trusted Christ?

   A. What changes did you see in your life, actions, attitude, problems? (Use specific examples.)

   B. How long did it take before you noticed changes?

   C. What personal benefits occurred?

Conclusion: What does Jesus Christ mean to you now?

DAY 5: USING EVANGELISTIC BIBLE STUDIES

Evangelistic Bible studies are a great tool to use with a group of neighbors or coworkers in a non-threatening environment. I have friends who regularly invite people to attend a 4-6 week Bible Study to learn about Jesus Christ. Each of these studies is developed to get people into the Word of God and to challenge them to look at who Jesus is and to consider their own response to Him. We only have time to look at one of these studies, but I am including other evangelistic studies at the end of today's lesson as resources for your spiritual toolbox. Ask God to give you an opportunity to use these evangelistic Bible studies with a group of people around you.

Today, I am going to use a different format, one which I often use when I lead small groups. It is the Hook, Book, Look, Took method. The HOOK is an opening question to get their interest. The BOOK is reading the passage. Then you LOOK at the passage to ask, what do I see, what does it mean? The TOOK is taking the information you have learned and applying it to your life. This is a great method to use when leading small groups.

Evangelistic Bible Study: The Most Important Question

Mark 10:17-27

HOOK:

- What is the greatest desire in your life? What do you want more than anything else?

- What would you be willing to give up for it?

BOOK: Read Mark 10:17-27.

LOOK:

1. Describe the man who came to Jesus.

2. What was his greatest desire?

3. What was Jesus' response to the man when he asked how to inherit eternal life?

4. Why did Jesus question the man for calling Him good? What was He trying to communicate here?

5. The man said he had kept all the commandments. Do you think the man had really kept all the commandments? Why or why not?

6. How does Jesus define keeping these commands? (See Matt. 5:21-22; 27-28).

7. Which of the 10 commandments does Jesus not mention? (See Exodus 20:3-17). Why do you think He doesn't mention them?

8. Back to the passage in Mark 10, why did Jesus feel love for this man?

9. What did Jesus tell the man to do? Why did Jesus ask him to do this?

10. What was the man's response? What did this reveal about the man? Which commands had he disobeyed now?

11. What was the man's basic presupposition about inheriting eternal life when he came to Jesus? What is wrong with his presupposition?

12. What were the presuppositions of the disciples when they asked, "Then who can be saved?"

TOOK:

- What do you consider the greatest cost to following Christ?

- What does Jesus promise to those who follow Him? If this promise is true, how would it affect your decision about following Christ?

- What is it in your life that would be hard for you to let go of in order to follow Christ?

- What have you learned from this passage that has impacted your life?

RESOURCES FOR YOU:

You can download other evangelistic Bible studies for free from my website www.crickettkeeth.com. Go to the Free Resources page and look for Evangelistic Bible studies. You can also download a blank testimony worksheet and other tools to use with those you're discipling.

Made in the USA
Las Vegas, NV
05 December 2023

82175271R00070